Charlie Chaplin

Copyright © 2015 by Quelle Histoire / quellehistoire.com
Published by Roaring Brook Press
Roaring Brook Press is a division of Holtzbrinck Publishing Holdings Limited Partnership
175 Fifth Avenue, New York, NY 10010
mackids.com

Library of Congress Control Number: 2017957513
ISBN 978-1-250-16623-4

Our books may be purchased in bulk for promotional, educational, or business use.
Please contact your local bookseller or the Macmillan Corporate and Premium Sales Department
at (800) 221-7945 ext. 5442 or by e-mail at MacmillanSpecialMarkets@macmillan.com.

First published in France in 2015 by Quelle Histoire, Paris
First U.S. edition, 2018

Text: Patricia Crété
Translation: Catherine Nolan
Illustrations: Bruno Wennagel, Mathieu Ferret, Aurélien Fernandez, Aurélie Verdon

Printed in China by RR Donnelley Asia Printing Solutions Ltd., Dongguan City, Guangdong Province
10 9 8 7 6 5 4 3 2 1

Charlie Chaplin

Roaring Brook Press
New York

Tough Start

Charlie Chaplin was one of the world's first big movie stars.

Charlie was born in 1889. He came from a poor family in London. His parents sang and danced in music halls there but without much success.

Charlie's father left the family when Charlie was small. Then his mother became ill. Charlie and his brother Sydney had to look out for themselves.

——

1889–1899

First Shows

To make money, the Chaplin boys started performing at a theater. At first, their boss thought Charlie was too shy to be onstage. But Charlie proved him wrong! Charlie played the piano. He tap-danced. He acted in funny plays.

He discovered that he was very, very good at making people laugh.

—

1900–1914

"The Tramp"

When Charlie was twenty-four years old, he moved to the United States. He started acting in movies. Back then, movies were silent. That meant there was no talking in them at all!

Charlie created a down-on-his-luck character called the Tramp. The Tramp wore baggy pants, big shoes, and a tiny mustache.

Audiences loved laughing at the Tramp's silly adventures. Charlie played him in many movies.

Before long, the Tramp was famous . . . and Charlie was, too!

———

1913–1915

Director

In 1918, Charlie had a chance to direct a movie. That meant he was in charge of all the actors and cameras.

Charlie starred in the movie, too. It was a comedy about World War I called *Shoulder Arms*.

The movie was a big hit. Charlie decided to make all his own movies from then on. That way they would be just the way he wanted.

—

1918

Modern Times

Charlie's movies were funny. But sometimes they had a serious message.

Charlie thought many factories were unfair to their workers. So he made the movie *Modern Times*. In the movie, the Tramp is a factory worker. He hurries to tighten nuts on a conveyor belt. The belt keeps moving faster and faster!

———

1936

The Great Dictator

Charlie made his first talking movie in 1939, *The Great Dictator*. It was another funny movie about something very serious.

In Europe, a cruel leader named Adolf Hitler was gaining power. Hitler happened to have a mustache that looked like the Tramp's.

Charlie put the Tramp in a Hitler outfit. He mocked Hitler's walk and talk. Charlie wanted to make Hitler look as foolish as possible.

——

1939–1940

A Big Family

In 1943, Charlie Chaplin married Oona O'Neill. It was his fourth time getting married!

Charlie said he had finally found his "perfect love." Charlie and Oona had eight children. One of them, Geraldine Chaplin, grew up to be a well-known actress.

___

1943

Limelight

Charlie's children got to act in a movie he made about his life. It's called *Limelight*.

After the movie was done, Charlie decided to move his family to Europe. The Chaplins boarded the ocean liner *Queen Elizabeth* in 1952. They sailed away to London and left America behind.

——

1952

Generosity

The Chaplins moved into a beautiful house in Switzerland. In 1954, the winter was bitter cold, and homeless people were dying in the streets.

Charlie remembered his poor childhood. He gave a huge sum of money to a priest who ran a charity that helped the homeless.

"I am not donating the money. I am returning it," said Charlie. "It belongs to my character the Tramp."

—————

1953–1954

Awards

Charlie's last movie was released in 1967. He had made more than eighty movies in all!

In 1972, he returned to the United States to accept a special Academy Award. He got a standing ovation—the longest one in the history of the Awards.

In 1975, he attended a grand ceremony at Buckingham Palace where Queen Elizabeth of England made him a knight! After that, he was called Sir Charlie Chaplin.

Charlie died at home in Switzerland in 1977, but his fame lives on.

1967–1977

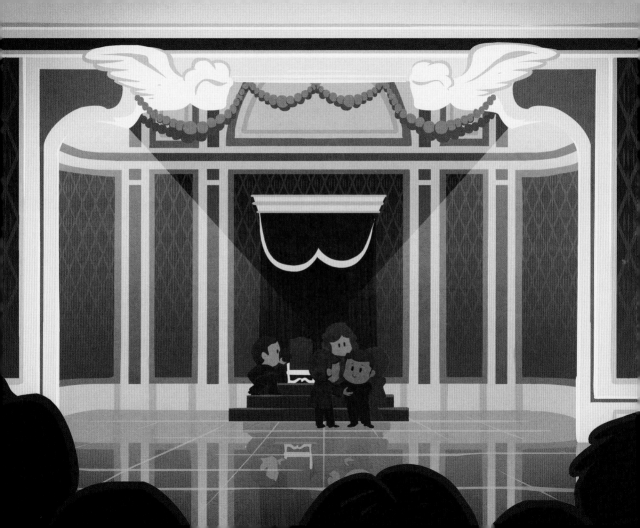

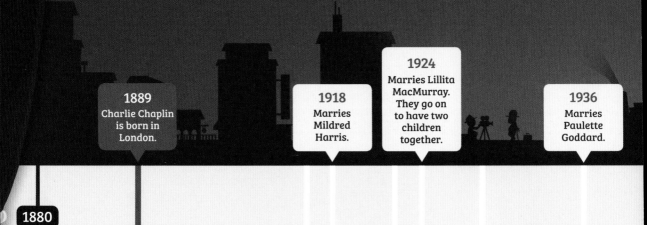

1889
Charlie Chaplin is born in London.

1918
Marries Mildred Harris.

1924
Marries Lillita MacMurray. They go on to have two children together.

1936
Marries Paulette Goddard.

1880

1914
Creates the character of the Tramp.

1921
Stars in a movie called *The Kid*.

1927
The start of movies with sound.

1943
Marries Oona O'Neill. They go on to have eight children together.

1952
Debut of the movie *Limelight*.

1964
Publishes a book about his life called *My Autobiography*.

1977
Dies in his sleep.

1980

1940
Makes *The Great Dictator*.

1952
Leaves the United States with his family.

1953
Settles in Switzerland.

1975
Knighted by Queen Elizabeth.

The United States and Europe

1 Walworth,
London, England

Charlie was born in this London neighborhood.

2 London Theater,
England

Charlie got his start here in 1909. Today it's home to the English National Opera.

3 Buckingham Palace,
London, England

The British royal family lives in this palace, built in 1703. Queen Elizabeth knighted Charlie here in 1975.

4 Hollywood,
Los Angeles, California

Charlie built his own movie studio in this Los Angeles neighborhood.

5 The Walk of Fame,
Los Angeles, California

More than 2,600 pink stars line Hollywood Boulevard, each one with the name of a show business celebrity on it. Charlie got his star in 1972.

6 Corsier-sur-Vevey,
Switzerland

Charlie and his family lived in this Swiss community on the shores of Lake Geneva. Now it's the site of a museum dedicated to Charlie's life and work.

People to Know

Fred Karno
(1866–1941)
This talent scout gave Charlie his first
break in show business.

Sydney Chaplin
(1885–1965)
Charlie's half brother stayed close
to him his whole life. He managed
Charlie's movie company, Charlie
Chaplin Productions.

Oona O'Neill
(1925–1991)
Oona's father was a famous playwright, Eugene O'Neill. She married Charlie Chaplin in 1943. They remained married until Charlie died.

Abbé Pierre
(1912–2007)
This priest started a charity in Switzerland to raise money for the homeless. Charlie gave the charity a large donation in 1954.

....

Charlie was pushed onstage
when he was five years old,
after his mother lost her voice
while she was singing.

....

Charlie kept making silent movies
long after other directors made
talking movies. In one of his films,
he poked fun at "talkies" by having
all the actors blow into kazoos
instead of saying real words.

....

Charlie was a perfectionist. He often filmed the same scene dozens of times until he got it right.

....

Charlie entered a Charlie Chaplin look-alike contest in 1975. He came in third!

Available Now

 Muhammad Ali

 Neil Armstrong

 Blackbeard

 Coco Chanel

 Charlie Chaplin

 Cleopatra

 Marie Curie

 Albert Einstein

 Abraham Lincoln

 Nelson Mandela

 Isaac Newton

 Rosa Parks

Coming Soon

 Anne Frank

 Gandhi

 Frida Kahlo

 Martin Luther King, Jr.